# The Anarcho Teachings of Yeshua

*Darryl W. Perry*

# The Anarcho Teachings of Yeshua

*Darryl W. Perry*

Published by Free Patriot Press
2010

ISBN: 0-9842037-2-9

ISBN 13: 978-0-9842037-2-7

## *Dedication:*

To the Creator (YHWH) for giving life & liberty.

To Jennifer Lokken & Jessica Pacholski for proof-reading, reviewing and being encouraging and supportive of this book.

To the rest of my friends and family for supporting me in all I do

# TOC

# Preface

When I began my research for this book, I was introduced to a philosophy called Anarcho-Theocracy, which is short on the anarcho yet heavy on Theocracy. It is not my intention to discuss or promote this philosophy. Instead my intention is to promote the anarcho teachings of Yeshua and dispel some of the myths regarding the teachings of Yeshua; namely the myths that those who follow His teaching (those calling themselves "Christians") should be subservient to the government and/or use governmental force to impose their beliefs/convictions on others.

# 2

# *What is Anarchy?*

Etymologically “anarchy” comes from the Medieval Latin anarchia, which comes from Greek anarchos (having no ruler), formed by the parts an-(no) + archos (ruler). A longer definition is “1) a : absence of government b : a state of lawlessness or political disorder due to the absence of governmental authority c : a utopian society of individuals who enjoy complete freedom without government.[1]”

Most people like to think that “anarchy” equals “chaos”, which is utterly false. Such an assumption leads one to believe that “order” comes from a government and denies the concepts of spontaneous order and a voluntaryist society. “The first thinker to articulate this modern concept of spontaneous order was Bernard de Mandeville, in a book called The Fable of the Bees (1714). This work discussed the paradox that “private vices” such as individual self-interest could lead to “public benefits” from which the whole community benefited. He observed that the sum of individuals acting

---

1 Merriam-Webster dictionary

from separate motives produced a commercial society that was no part of any one person's intention. This idea that the evolution of human institutions allowed individuals to serve others, even though their motive might be self-interest, was at the core of the Scottish Enlightenment that grew up around Adam Smith, David Hume, and Adam Ferguson. They sought to apply this idea to a whole range of human institutions, including commerce, law, language, human morality, and even mores and customs. Far from a narrow theory of economics, Smith's Theory of Moral Sentiments (1759) argued that morals evolved slowly. The principles that enabled humanity to flourish and prosper were eventually accepted by the community. They stood the test of time...Hayek took on the ancient idea that institutions were divided between those that are "natural" and those that are "artificial." A third group existed, Hayek said, and these were social institutions. As these are regular and orderly, people suppose that they have been invented by humanity and can therefore be altered or restructured at will. Hayek pointed out that this notion was mistaken because the human mind and society had evolved together. Tearing down the institutions that kept society together and building anew, as socialists advocated, would destroy the order that made society work...Spontaneous order keeps the wheels of society turning without the need to issue commands from the center. **A free society is orderly not because people are told what to do** but because the evolving traditions and inherited institutions of human society allow individuals to pursue their own ends and by so doing, meet the needs of others.[2]"

This is not a completely secular concept. One need only read the Hebrew Scriptures to see that from the time of the Exodus from Egypt until the coronation of King Saul, the Hebrew people lived in an anarchist society. "And the sons of Israel went up and down from there at that time, each to his tribe, and to his family. And they departed from there, every man to his inheritance. In those days there was no king in Israel. Each man did that which was right in his own eyes.[3]" That is the epitome of freedom and natural liberty. "The power of acting as one thinks fit, without any restraint or control, unless by the law of nature. The right which nature gives to all mankind of disposing of their persons and

---

2 By Nigel Ashford
The Freeman July 1999 Volume: 49 Issue: 7

3 Judges 21:24-25 (LITV)

property after the manner they judge most consistent with their happiness, on condition of their acting with an equal exercise of the same rights by other men. It is called by Lieber social liberty", and is defined as the protection or unrestrained action in as high a degree as the same claim of protection of each individual admits of.[4]"

4 Black's Law Dictionary, Revised Fourth Edition, 1968

# 7

# Non-Aggression:
## The Greatest Commandment

"...And one of them, a lawyer, questioned Him, testing Him, and saying, "Teacher, which is the great commandment in the Law?" And Yeshua said to him, "You shall love the Lord your God with all your heart, and with all your soul, and with all your mind."[5] This is the first and great commandment. And the second is like it: "You shall love your neighbor as yourself."[6] On these two commandments all the Law and the Prophets hang." [7]

"... I give a new commandment to you, that you should love one another; according as I loved you, you should also love one another. By this all shall know that you are My

---

5 Deuteronomy. 6:5
6 Leviticus 19:18
7 Mathew 22:35-40 (LITV)

disciples, if you have love among one another."[8]

A recurring theme in the teachings of Yeshua,is love. But, what is "love"? The Apostle Paul wrote to the Corinthians, "Love has patience, is kind; love is not envious; love is not vain, is not puffed up; does not behave indecently, does not pursue its own things, is not easily provoked, thinks no evil; does not rejoice in unrighteousness, but rejoices in the truth. Love quietly covers all things, believes all things, hopes all things, endures all things."[9] In short, if we are loving towards others, we are not being judgmental and we are following the teachings of Yeshua, who warns, "Do not judge, that you may not be judged; for with whatever judgment you judge, you will be judged; and with whatever measure you measure, it will be measured again to you."[10] Saying, "do not judge", is not speaking to not judging at all -- it is speaking to not judging unfairly. This philosophy is again reiterated when Yeshua teaches, "Therefore, all things, whatever you desire

8 John 13:34-35 (LITV)
9 1 Corinthians 13: 4-7 (LITV)
10 Matthew 7:1-2 (LITV)

that men should do to you, so also you should do to them; for this is the Law and the Prophets."[11] This one sentence sums up the two greatest commandments, "love YHWH and love your neighbor" and the new commandment given by Yeshua at the Last Supper, "you should love one another; according as I loved you."

Some claim that it is unachievable to love everyone. Yet, Yeshua lived what He taught, "that we must keep our hearts free from resentment, no matter how we may be mistreated...to practice the Golden Rule, even in small measure, makes us happy, helps us in our business, and in every relation of life. IT IS THE MOST PRACTICAL THING IN THE WORLD."[12](emphasis added)

If following the Golden Rule is the most "practical thing in the world" for an individual, why do so many people make exceptions for the group? The individual doesn't have a right to take from his neighbor. However, most followers of Yeshua concede that a group known as "the government" DOES have that right. What is the difference?

---

11 Matthew 7:12 (LITV)
The "Golden Rule" commonly worded, "do unto others as you would have them do unto you"

12 Halley's Bible Handbook Twenty-Fourth Edition pg 501

Yeshua, doesn't make a distinction or exception between the individual and the group. Many “Christians” claim the exception comes, not from Yeshua, but from the Apostle Paul's letter to the church in Rome, “Let every soul be subject to higher authorities, for there is no authority except from God, but the existing authorities have been ordained by God. So that the one resisting authority has opposed the ordinance of God, and the ones opposing will receive judgment to themselves.”[13]

Chuck Baldwin asks, “Do our Christian friends who use these verses to teach that we should not oppose any political leader really believe that civil magistrates have unlimited authority to do anything they want without opposition? I doubt that they truly believe that.

For example, what if our President decided to resurrect the old monarchal custom of Jus Primae Noctis (Law of First Night)? That was the old medieval custom when the king claimed the right to sleep with a subject's bride on the first night of their marriage. Would our sincere Christian brethren sheepishly say, "Romans Chapter 13

---

13 Romans 13:1-2 (LITV)

says we must submit to the government"? I think not. And would any of us respect any man who would submit to such a law? I wouldn't.

So, there are limits to authority. A father has authority in his home, but does this give him power to abuse his wife and children? Of course not. An employer has authority on the job, but does this give him power to control the private lives of his employees? No. A pastor has overseer authority in the church, but does this give him power to tell employers in his church how to run their businesses? Of course not. All human authority is limited in nature. No man has unlimited authority over the lives of other men."[14]

You see, the group has no authority not given to the individual. The group should also, collectively, practice "love towards one another", for Yeshua tells us, "on these commandments (love YHWH and love your neighbor) all the Law and the Prophets hang". The Law (or Torah), in Judaism, is more than the Ten Commandments, it's the entirety of the first five books of the Bible (Genesis,

---

14 Chuck Baldwin Live http://www.chuckbaldwinlive.com/c2009/cbarchive_20090227.html

Exodus, Leviticus, Numbers, Deuteronomy). Yet, Yeshua, "fulfilled the Law"[15] that we may be free.[16] Through the grace of YHWH, we are free from the Law, but this freedom from the law is not a license to do as we please. We are still commanded to "love one another." This is the basis of the non-aggression principle, "that no one has the right, under any circumstances, to initiate force against another human being for any reason whatever; nor advocate the initiation of force, or delegate it to anyone else."

Yeshua taught in one of His first (and most famous) public sermons, "Blessed are the meek...Blessed are the merciful...Blessed are the pure in heart...Blessed are the peacemakers!"[17] If Yeshua consistently preached mercy, love and peace; how can those who claim to follow His teachings promote indifference, hatred and war?

---

15 Matthew 5:17 (LITV)
16 John 8:31-36
17 Matthew 5:5-9 (LITV)

13

# *Render unto Caesar:*
## *An Argument Against Central Banking*

"...the Pharisees took counsel so as they might trap Him in words. And they sent to Him their disciples with the Herodians, saying, "Teacher, we know that You are true, and teach the way of God in truth, and it does not concern You about anyone, for You do not look to the face of men. Then tell us, what do You think? Is it lawful to give tribute to Caesar, or not?"

But knowing their wickedness, Yeshua said, "Why do you test Me, hypocrites? Show Me the tribute coin."

And they brought a denarius to Him. And He said to them, "Whose image and inscription is this?"

They said to Him, "Caesar's."

Then He said to them, "Then give to Caesar

the things of Caesar, and to God the things of God.""[18]

Most churches use this passage of Scripture to teach their congregation to pay taxes, after all the "money" we use comes from our version of Caesar. However, that's not the message being taught by Yeshua. In order to understand the entire context of this passage, one must understand the context of the times as well.

During the life of Yeshua, as with the vast majority of history of mankind, there was no "Central Bank" that printed money. Certainly, Caesar - along with other kings, princes and governors - issued coins that could be used throughout the empire, but to supplement (or compete with the "kings money") there were several alternative and local currencies. (The Temple, for example had it's own currency, that could only be used at the Temple and explains the reason for the money-changers.)In this case, His accuser gave him a Roman coin with the inscription of Caesar, most likely Tiberius. It is perhaps significant

---

18 Matthew22:15-22 (LITV)
see also Mark 12:13-17 & Luke 20:20-26

that Yeshua did not have such a coin with him but that one of his questioners did.

Yeshua answered, “Render unto Caesar the things that are Caesar's and to YHWH the things that are YHWH's”

“In context, the saying is thoroughly ambiguous. The word "render" means "give back." The first half of the saying could thus mean, "It's Caesar's coin--go ahead and give it back to him."...When its second half is added, the phrase remains equally ambiguous. What belongs to Caesar, and what belongs to God? The possible answers range from "Pay your tribute tax to Caesar, and your temple tax to God" to "Everything belongs to God." If the latter, what is owed to Caesar? Nothing.”[19]

“With this answer (“Render unto Causear what is Caesar's and to YHWH what is YHWH's) Yeshua does not say that taxes are lawful. He does not counsel obedience to the Romans. He simply faces up to the evidence.”[20] Even if one rejects the idea that all things belong to YHWH, they are forced to acknowledge that governments own/create nothing that they

19 Marcus Borg Beliefnet.com http://www.beliefnet.com/Faiths/2000/04/What-Belongs-To-God.aspx

20 Anarchy and Christianity by Jacques Elul pg 60

did not first take from someone else. I can think of no better argument from the Scriptures to oppose "Central Banks" and taxation than this.

But what is a "Central Bank"? "A central bank is the term used to describe the authority responsible for policies that affect a country's supply of money and credit. More specifically, a central bank uses its tools of monetary policy—open market operations, discount window lending, changes in reserve requirements—to affect short-term interest rates and the monetary base (currency held by the public plus bank reserves) and to achieve important policy goals.[21]"

The Federal Reserve (the current Central Bank in the United States of America) claims, "to provide the nation with a safer, more flexible, and more stable monetary and financial system." Yet, "throughout its nearly 100-year history, the Federal Reserve has presided over the near-complete destruction of the United States dollar. Since 1913 the dollar has lost over 95% of its purchasing power, aided and abetted by the Federal

---

21 A Brief History of Central Banks by Michael D. Bordo http://clevelandfed.org/research/commentary/2007/12.cfm

Reserve's loose monetary policy.[22]" Ron Paul says governing authorities have used coercion "to force their citizens to accept debased and devalued currency. Gresham's Law describes this phenomenon, which can be summed up in one phrase: bad money drives out good money. An emperor, a king, or a dictator might mint coins with half an ounce of gold and force merchants, under pain of death, to accept them as though they contained one ounce of gold. Each ounce of the king's gold could now be minted into two coins instead of one, so the king now had twice as much "money" to spend on building castles and raising armies. As these legally overvalued coins circulated, the coins containing the full ounce of gold would be pulled out of circulation and hoarded....These actions also give rise to the most pernicious effects of inflation....In the absence of legal tender laws, Gresham's Law no longer holds. If people are free to reject debased currency, and instead demand sound money, sound money will gradually return to use in society. Merchants would have been free to reject the king's coin and accept only coins containing full metal weight."

---

22 Ron Paul (February 26, 2009) http://ronpaul.com/on-the-issues/audit-the-federal-reserve-hr-1207

Without legal tender laws, a “central bank”, printing press, or coin mint, the Caesars of our day have nothing. If Caesar has nothing – “whatever does not bear Caesar's mark does not belong to him”[23] - he cannot be owed anything...and there would be nothing for us to “render unto Caesar.”

23 Anarchy and Christianity by Jacques Elul pg 60

19

# *Property, Contracts & Free Will:*

"A housemaster, who went out when it was early to hire workers into his vineyard. And agreeing with the workers for a denarius for the day, he sent them into his vineyard. And going out about the third hour, he saw others standing idle in the market. And he said to them, "You also go into the vineyard, and I will give you whatever is just."

And they went. Again, going out about the sixth and ninth hour, he did the same. And going out about the eleventh hour, he found others standing idle, and said to them, "Why do you stand here idle all day?"

They said to him, "Because no one has hired us."

He said to them, "You also go into the vineyard, and you will receive whatever is just."

But evening having come, the lord of the vineyard said to his manager, "Call the workers and pay them the wage, beginning from the last to the first."

And the ones having come the eleventh hour each received a denarius. And having come, the first supposed that they would receive more. And they also each received a denarius. And having received it, they murmured against the housemaster, saying, "These last have performed one hour, and you have made them equal to us who have borne the burden and the heat of the day."

But answering, he said to one of them, "Friend, I do not wrong you. Did you not agree to a denarius with me? Take yours and go. But I desire to give to this last as also to you. Or is it not lawful for me to do what I desire with my things? Or is your eye evil because I am good?"'"[24]

In this "Parable of the Workers in the Vineyard", Yeshua is teaching an important lesson to His followers specifically concerning the "rewards" they will receive in the after-life, that all are rewarded equally. But parables, much like prophesy, usually have multiple meanings. A literal interpretation of this parable teaches a commonly understood concept of contracts. The owner of the vineyard made a contract with the workers. The first group were contracted for a "denarius" which was a "days wage," the remaining workers were told they would "receive whatever is just." At the end of the day the owner, in accordance with the Torah,[25] paid his workers -beginning with those hired last. Being a just man, he paid all of his workers a day's wage. The workers hired at the beginning of the day complained, not because of what they received, but instead saying, "These last have performed one hour, and you have made them equal to us.[26]" He answered them, "Friend, I do not

---

24 Mathew 20:1-15 (LITV)
25 Leviticus 19:13; Deuteronomy 24:15
26 Matthew 20:11-12

wrong you. Did you not agree to a denarius with me? Take yours and go. But I desire to give to this last as also to you. Or is it not lawful for me to do what I desire with my things? Or is your eye evil because I am good?[27]"

It is with his reply that he proves the binding nature of their contract. The first workers agreed to work for a days wage - each party held his end of the contract. The land owner then asks two more questions, the first relating to free will, "is it not lawful for me to do what I desire with my things?[28]" The second a more general question regarding the worker's attitude, "Or is your eye evil because I am good?[29]"

As Lew Rockwell explains,"If the free market works—meaning the existence of exchange under private property and contract enforcement—then there is no need for such laws; indeed, such laws do violence to the market.[30]" There was no breach of contract and no need for an arbiter, so the "free market" worked. Perhaps, the disgruntled

27 Matthew 20:13-15
28 Matthew 20:15
29 Matthew 20:15
30 Lew Rockwell "The Bridge of Asses" http://mises.org/story/1344

workers are the type of person mentioned by Dr. Walter E. Williams, "Freedom of contract has come to be viewed with contempt. Suppose you offer to pay me for $3 an hour and I agree; suppose I live in Virginia and want to purchase liquor in Washington, D.C.; suppose in rent-controlled New York and San Francisco a landlord and tenant mutually agree to pay a higher rent; suppose I'm a California navel orange grower who wants to sell his entire crop; and suppose you want to provide taxi services in New York but don't have $170,000 for a license. There are literally thousands of restrictions like these on freedom of contract. You might say, "Williams, there are good reasons for restricting the freedoms of others." You're right, and every tyrant who has ever existed has had what he considered a good reason.[31]"

The second question, "is it not lawful for me to do what I desire with my things?[32]" is much more complicated to answer from a theological perspective. However, from the anarcho perspective the answer is obvious, "yes, you have the right to do as you desire

---

31 Walter E. Williams "Threats to the Rule of Law in America" http://www.capmag.com/article.asp?id=1694

32 Matthew 20:13-15

with your things". There are some that falsely deny that man has free will and indeed many books have been written on the subject. But one does not need a government, only voluntary association, to ensure contracts and property are protected.

# Civil Disobedience:

## The Trials of Yeshua

Perhaps the most over looked teaching of Yeshua would be His acts of civil disobedience. The most obvious of these acts involves the picking/eating of grain on the Sabbath. “At that time on the sabbath, Yeshua went through the grain fields. And His disciples were hungry, and began to pluck heads of grain and to eat. But seeing, the Pharisees said to Him, “Behold, your disciples are doing what it is not lawful to do on the sabbath.” But He said to them, “Have you not read what David did, when he and those with him hungered? How he entered into the house of God, and he ate the Loaves of the Presentation, which it was not lawful for him to eat, nor for those with him, but for the priests only? Or have you not read in the Law that on the sabbaths the priests in the temple profane the sabbath and are guiltless? But I say to you, One greater than the temple is here. But if you had known what this is, "I desire mercy and not sacrifice,"[33] you would not have condemned the guiltless. For the Son of Man is also Lord of the sabbath.[34]"

The Hebrew Law was strict about "working" on the Sabbath, but Jewish tradition had added restrictions to the point of voiding the original intent. Not to mention that His claim of being "Lord of the Sabbath" was equivalent to a claim of Diety.[35] It was this claim that led the Pharisees and Sanhedrin to eventually arrest Yeshua and have him put to death. It is during these trials, one before the Sanhedrin and one before Pilate, that Yeshua's civil disobedience can best be seen.

Some theologians argue that since Yeshua "agreed" to be tried before Pilate, that He recognized and submitted to his authority, and thus regarded Pilate's authority as legitimate. This is not necessarily the case. Yeshua's attitude during the trial is consistent, but is shown in various forms: silence, accusation of authorities or deliberate provocation.[36]

---

33 Hos. 6:6
34 Matthew 12:1-8 (LITV)
35 Halley's Bible Handbook Twenty-Fourth Edition pg 463
36 Anarchy and Christianity by Jacques Elul pg 65-67

Yeshua is first accused of saying he would destroy the Temple. He remained silent. Again, in front of Pilate, Yeshua faced many accusations and remained silent. This is not because He was being submissive to their perceived authority, but perhaps because he knew that the trial would not bring justice and felt no need to defend himself.

He even takes a jab at his accusers, first when they arrest Him, "Have you come out to take Me with swords and clubs, as against a plunderer? I sat with you daily teaching in the temple, and you did not lay hands on Me.[37]" Then before the High Priest, "Then the high priest questioned Yeshua about His disciples and about His doctrine. Yeshua answered him, "I publicly spoke to the world; I always taught in the synagogue and in the temple where the Jews always come together, and I spoke nothing in secret. Why do you question Me? Question those hearing what I spoke to them: behold, these know what I said!"[38]" And lastly when tried before Pilate, "Pilate said to Him, "Do You not speak to me? Do You not know that I have authority to crucify You, and I have authority to release You?" Yeshua answered, "You would have no authority

---

37 Mathew 22:55 (LITV)
38 John 18:19-21 (LITV)

against Me, not any, if it were not given to you from above. Because of this, the one delivering Me to you has a greater sin."[39]" Some claim that Yeshua is telling Pilate that his authority comes from YHWH, but if we look at the temptation of Yeshua in the wilderness, we see that earthly power comes from Lucifer[40].

Lastly, we find provocation on the part of the Messiah. When He is facing the High Priest, "the high priest said to Him, "I put You on oath by the living God that You tell us if You are the Christ, the Son of God." Yeshua said to him, "You said it. I tell you more. From this time you shall see the Son of Man sitting off the right hand of power, and coming on the clouds of the heaven.[41]" He never calls himself the "Messiah" or the "son of YHWH", only "the Son of Man" (i.e. true man).[42] Next, Yeshua uses provocation with Pilate, "Pilate again went into the praetorium and called Yeshua, and said to Him, "Are You the King of the Jews?" Yeshua answered him, "Do you say this from yourself, or did others tell you about Me?" Pilate answered, "Not,

39 John 19:10-11 (LITV)
40 Matthew 4:8
41 Mathew 26:63-64
42 Anarchy and Christianity by Jacques Elul pg 70

am I a Jew? Your nation, even the chief priests, delivered You up to me! What did You do?" Yeshua answered, "My kingdom is not of this world. If My kingdom were of this world, My servants would have fought that I might not be delivered up to the Jews. But now My kingdom is not from here." Then Pilate said to Him, "Are You really a king?" Yeshua answered, "You say that I am a king. For this purpose I have been born, and for this I have come into the world, that I might witness to the Truth. Everyone being of the Truth hears My voice."[43]

During the trials of Yeshua, with both political and religious authorities, He answers with a mix of irony, scorn, non-cooperation, indifference and sometimes accusation, but always knowing that they have no real authority over Him.

---

43 John 18:33-37 (LITV)

# Appendix A
# The "Christmas" Story

There was in the days of Herod, the king of Judea, a certain priest named Zacharias, of the division of Abijah. His wife was of the daughters of Aaron, and her name was Elizabeth. And they were both righteous before God, walking in all the commandments and ordinances of YHWH blameless. But they had no child, because Elizabeth was barren, and they were both well advanced in years. So it was, that while he was serving as priest before God in the order of his division, according to the custom of the priesthood, his lot fell to burn incense when he went into the temple of YHWH. And the whole multitude of the people was praying outside at the hour of incense. Then an angel of YHWH appeared to him, standing on the right side of the altar of incense. And when Zacharias saw him, he was troubled, and fear fell upon him.

The angel Gabriel said, "Do not be afraid, Zacharias, for your prayer is heard; and your wife Elizabeth will bear you a son, and you shall call his name John. And you will have joy and gladness, and many will rejoice at his birth. For he will be great in the sight of YHWH, and shall drink neither wine nor strong drink. He will also be filled with the Holy Spirit, even from his mother's womb. And he will turn many of the children of Israel to YHWH their God. He will also go before Him in the spirit and power of Elijah, 'to turn the hearts of the fathers to the children,' and the disobedient to the wisdom of the just, to make ready a people prepared for YHWH."

Zacharias asked, "How shall I know this? For I am an old man, and my wife is well advanced in years."

The angel replied, "I am Gabriel, who stands in the presence of God, and was sent to speak to you and bring you these glad tidings. But behold, you will be mute and not able to speak until the day these things take place, because you did not believe my words which will be fulfilled in their own time."

And the people waited for Zacharias, and marveled that he lingered so long in the temple. But when he came out, he could not speak to them; and they perceived that he had seen a vision in the temple, for he beckoned to them and remained speechless. And so it was, as soon as the days of his service were completed, that he departed to his own house. Now after those days his wife Elizabeth conceived; and she hid herself five months,

Elizabeth said, "Thus YHWH has dealt with me, in the days when He looked on me, to take away my reproach among people."

Now in the sixth month the angel Gabriel was sent by God to a city of Galilee named Nazareth, to a virgin betrothed to a man whose name was Joseph, of the house of David. The virgin's name was Mary. And having come in, the angel Gabriel said to her, "Rejoice, highly favored one, YHWH is with you; blessed are you among women!"

But when she saw him, she was troubled at his saying, and considered what manner of greeting this was. "Do not be afraid, Mary, for you have found favor with God. And behold, you will conceive in your womb and bring forth a Son, and shall call His name Yeshua. He will be great, and will be called the Son of the Highest; and YHWH God will give Him the throne of His father David. And He will reign over the house of Jacob forever, and of His kingdom there will be no end."

Mary asked, "How can this be, since I do not know a man?"

The angel Gabriel replied, "The Holy Spirit will come upon you, and the power of the Highest will overshadow you; therefore, also, that Holy One who is to be born will be called the Son of God. Now indeed, Elizabeth your relative has also conceived a son in her old age; and this is now the sixth month for her who was called barren. For with God nothing will be impossible."

"Behold the maidservant of YHWH! Let it be to me according to your word."

And the angel departed from her.

Now Mary arose in those days and went into the hill country with haste, to a city of Judah, and entered the house of Zacharias and greeted Elizabeth. And it happened, when Elizabeth heard the greeting of Mary, that the babe leaped in her womb; and Elizabeth was filled with the Holy Spirit. Then she spoke out with a loud voice, "Blessed are you among women, and blessed is the fruit of your womb! But why is this granted to me, that the mother of my YHWH should come to me? For indeed, as soon as the voice of your greeting sounded in my ears, the babe leaped in my womb for joy. Blessed is she who believed, for there will be a fulfillment of those things which were told her from YHWH."

Mary said, "My soul magnifies YHWH, And my spirit has rejoiced in God my Savior. For He has regarded the lowly state of His maidservant; For behold, henceforth all generations will call me blessed. For He who is mighty has done great things for me, And holy is His name. And His mercy is on those who fear Him From generation to generation. He has shown strength with His arm; He has scattered the proud in the imagination of their hearts. He has put down the mighty from their thrones, And exalted the lowly. He has filled the hungry with good things, And the rich He has sent away empty. He has helped His servant Israel, In remembrance of His mercy, As He spoke to our fathers, To Abraham and to his seed forever."

And Mary remained with her about three months, and returned to her house. Then Joseph her husband, being a just man, and not wanting to make her a public example, was minded to put her away secretly. But while he thought about these things, behold, an angel of YHWH appeared to him in a dream, saying, "Joseph, son of David, do not be afraid to take to you Mary your wife, for that which is conceived in her is of the Holy Spirit. And she will bring forth a Son, and you shall call His name Yeshua, for He will save His people from their sins."

So all this was done that it might be fulfilled which was spoken by YHWH through the prophet, saying: "Behold, the virgin shall be with child, and bear a Son, and they shall call His name Immanuel," which is translated, "God with us." Then Joseph, being aroused from sleep, did as the angel of YHWH commanded him and took to him his wife, and did not know her till she had brought forth her firstborn Son. And it came to pass in those days that a decree went out from Caesar Augustus that all the world should be registered. This census first took place while Quirinius was governing Syria. So all went to be registered, everyone to his own city. Joseph also went up from Galilee, out of the city of Nazareth, into Judea, to the city of David, which is called Bethlehem, because he was of the house and lineage of David, to be registered with Mary, his betrothed wife, who was with child.

So it was, that while they were there, the days were completed for her to be delivered. And she brought forth her firstborn Son, and wrapped Him in swaddling cloths, and laid Him in a manger, because there was no room for them in the inn.

Now there were in the same country shepherds living out in the fields, keeping watch over their flock by night. And behold, an angel of YHWH stood before them, and the glory of YHWH shone around them, and they were greatly afraid.

The angel said to them, "Do not be afraid, for behold, I bring you good tidings of great joy which will be to all people. For there is born to you this day in the city of David a Savior, who is Christ YHWH. And this will be the sign to you: You will find a Babe wrapped in swaddling cloths, lying in a manger."

And suddenly there was with the angel a multitude of the heavenly host praising God and saying, "Glory to God in the highest, And on earth peace, goodwill toward men!"

So it was, when the angels had gone away from them into heaven, that the shepherds said to one another, "Let us now go to Bethlehem and see this thing that has come to pass, which YHWH has made known to us."

And they came with haste and found Mary and Joseph, and the Babe lying in a manger. Now when they had seen Him, they made widely known the saying which was told them concerning this Child. And all those who heard it marveled at those things which were told them by the shepherds. But Mary kept all these things and pondered them in her heart. Then the shepherds returned, glorifying and praising God for all the things that they had heard and seen, as it was told them.

Now after Yeshua was born in Bethlehem of Judea in the days of Herod the king, behold, wise men from the East came to Jerusalem asking, "Where is He who has been born King of the Jews? For we have seen His star in the East and have come to worship Him."

When Herod the king heard this, he was troubled, and all Jerusalem with him. And when he had gathered all the chief priests and scribes of the people together, he inquired of them where the Christ was to be born.

The wise men replied, "In Bethlehem of Judea, for thus it is written by the prophet: 'But you, Bethlehem, in the land of Judah, Are not the least among the rulers of Judah; For out of you shall come a Ruler Who will shepherd My people Israel.'"

Then Herod, when he had secretly called the wise men, determined from them what time the star appeared. And he sent them to Bethlehem and said, "Go and search carefully for the young Child, and when you have found Him, bring back word to me, that I may come and worship Him also."

When they heard the king, they departed; and behold, the star which they had seen in the East went before them, till it came and stood over where the young Child was. When they saw the star, they rejoiced with exceedingly great joy. And when they had come into the house, they saw the young

Child with Mary His mother, and fell down and worshiped Him. And when they had opened their treasures, they presented gifts to Him: gold, frankincense, and myrrh. Then, being divinely warned in a dream that they should not return to Herod, they departed for their own country another way.

Now when the days of her purification according to the law of Moses were completed, they brought Him to Jerusalem to present Him to YHWH (as it is written in the law of YHWH, "Every male who opens the womb shall be called holy to YHWH"), and to offer a sacrifice according to what is said in the law of YHWH, "A pair of turtledoves or two young pigeons." And behold, there was a man in Jerusalem whose name was Simeon, and this man was just and devout, waiting for the Consolation of Israel, and the Holy Spirit was upon him. And it had been revealed to him by the Holy Spirit that he would not see death before he had seen YHWH's Christ. So he came by the Spirit into the temple. And when the parents brought in the Child, to do for Him according to the custom of the law, he took Him up in his arms and blessed God saying, "YHWH, now You are letting Your servant depart in peace, According to Your word; For my eyes have seen Your salvation Which You have prepared before the face of all peoples, A light to bring revelation to the Gentiles, And the glory of Your people Israel."

And Joseph and His mother marveled at those things which were spoken of Him. Then Simeon blessed them, and said to Mary His mother, "Behold, this Child is destined for the fall and rising of many in Israel, and for a sign which will be spoken against (yes, a sword will pierce through your own soul also), that the thoughts of many hearts may be revealed."

Now there was one, Anna, a prophetess, the daughter of Phanuel, of the tribe of Asher. She was of a great age, and had lived with a husband seven years from her virginity; and this woman was a widow of about eighty-four years, who did not depart from the temple, but served God with fastings and prayers night and day. And coming in that instant she gave thanks to YHWH, and spoke of Him to all those who looked for redemption in Jerusalem. So when they had performed all things according to the law of YHWH, they returned to Galilee, to their own city, Nazareth. And the Child grew and became strong in spirit, filled with wisdom; and the grace of God was upon Him.

Now when they had departed, behold, an angel of YHWH appeared to Joseph in a dream, saying, "Arise, take the young Child and His mother, flee to Egypt, and stay there until I bring you word; for Herod will seek the young Child to destroy Him."

When he arose, he took the young Child and His mother by night and departed for Egypt, and was there until the death of Herod, that it might be fulfilled which was spoken by YHWH through the prophet, saying, "Out of Egypt I called My Son." Then Herod, when he saw that he was deceived by the wise men, was exceedingly angry; and he sent forth and put to death all the male children who were in Bethlehem and in all its districts, from two years old and under, according to the time which he had determined from the wise men. Then was fulfilled what was spoken by Jeremiah the prophet, saying: "A voice was heard in Ramah, Lamentation, weeping, and great mourning, Rachel weeping for her children, Refusing to be comforted, Because they are no more." But when Herod was dead, behold, an angel of YHWH appeared in a dream to Joseph in Egypt saying,, "Arise, take the young Child and His mother, and go to the land of Israel, for those who sought the young Child's life are dead."

Then he arose, took the young Child and His mother, and came into the land of Israel. But when he heard that Archelaus was reigning over Judea instead of his father Herod, he was afraid to go there. And being warned by God in a dream, he turned aside into the region of Galilee. And he came and dwelt in a city called Nazareth, that it might be fulfilled which was spoken by the prophets, "He shall be called a Nazarene."

# Appendix B
# The "Easter" Story

He said to His disciples, "You know that the Passover is coming after two days, and the Son of Man is betrayed to be crucified."

Then the chief priests and the scribes and the elders of the people were assembled to the court of the high priest, the one named Caiaphas. And they plotted together in order that they might seize Yeshua by guile and kill Him. But they said, "Not during the Feast, that there be no turmoil among the people."

And Yeshua being in Bethany, in Simon the leper's house, a woman came to Him having an alabaster vial of ointment, very precious. And she poured it on His head as He reclined. But seeing, His disciples were indignant, saying, "For what is this waste? For this ointment could have been sold for much and be given to the poor."

But knowing, Yeshua said to them, "Why do you cause trouble to the woman? For she worked a good work toward Me. For you always have the poor with you, but you do not always have Me. For in putting this ointment on My body, she did it in order to bury Me. Truly I say to you, Wherever this gospel is proclaimed in all the world, what she did will be spoken of for a memorial of her."

Then one of the twelve going to the chief priests, the one called Judas Iscariot, said, "What will you give to me, and I will deliver Him up to you?" And they weighed to him thirty silver pieces. And from then he sought opportunity that he might betray Him.

And on the first day of the Feast of Unleavened Bread, the disciples came to Yeshua, "saying to Him, Where do you desire we should prepare for You to eat the Passover?"

And He said, "Go into the city to a certain one and say to him, 'The Teacher says, My time is near; toward you I will prepare the Passover with My disciples.'"

And the disciples did as Yeshua ordered them, and prepared the Passover. And evening having come, He reclined with the Twelve. And as they were eating, He said, "Truly I say to you that one of you will betray Me."

And grieving exceedingly, they began to say to Him, each of them, "Lord, not at all I is it?" But answering, He said, "The one dipping the hand with Me in the dish will betray Me. Indeed, the Son of Man goes, as it has been written about Him. But woe to that man by whom the Son of Man is betrayed. It were good for him if that man was never born."

And answering, the one betraying Him, Judas, said, "Not at all I is it, Rabbi?"

He said to him, "You have said it."

And as they ate, taking the bread and blessing it, Yeshua broke and gave to the disciples, and said, "Take, eat; this is My body. And taking the cup, and giving thanks," He gave to them, saying, "Drink all of it. For this is My blood of the New Covenant which concerning many is being poured out for remission of sins. But I say to you, I will not at all drink of this fruit of the vine after this until that day when I drink it new with you in the kingdom of My Father."

And singing a hymn, they went to the Mount of Olives. Then Yeshua said to them, "You all will be offended in Me during this night. For it has been written, "I will smite the Shepherd, and the sheep of the flock will be scattered." But after My resurrection I will go before you into Galilee."

Then Yeshua came with them to a place called Gethsemane. And He said to the disciples, "Sit here, until going away, I shall pray there."

And taking along Peter and the two sons of Zebedee, He began to grieve and to be deeply troubled. Then He said to them, “My soul is deeply grieved, even unto death. Stay here and watch with Me.”

And going forward a little, He fell on His face, praying, and saying, “My Father, if it is possible, let this cup pass from Me; yet not as I will, but as You will.”

And He came to the disciples and found them sleeping. And He said to Peter, “So! Were you not able to watch one hour with Me? Watch and pray, that you do not enter into temptation. The spirit indeed is eager, but the flesh is weak.” Again, going away a second time,

He prayed, saying, “My Father, if it is not possible for this cup to pass away except I drink it, let Your will be done.” And coming, He again found them sleeping, for their eyes were heavy. And leaving them, going away again, He prayed a third time, saying the same word. Then He came to His disciples and said to them, “Sleep on, and rest for what time remains. Behold, the hour draws near, and the Son of Man is betrayed into the hands of sinners. Rise up, let us go. Behold, the one betraying Me draws near.”

And as He was yet speaking, behold, Judas came, one of the Twelve. And with him was a numerous crowd with swords and clubs, from the chief priests and elders of the people. And the one betraying Him gave them a sign, saying, “Whomever I may kiss, it is He; seize Him.” And coming up at once to Yeshua, he said, “Hail, Rabbi.”

And he ardently kissed Him. But Yeshua said to him, “Friend, why are you here?”

Then coming up, they laid hands on Yeshua and seized Him. And, behold, one of those with Yeshua, stretching out the hand, drew his sword and struck the slave of the high priest and took off his ear. Then Yeshua said to him, “Put your sword back into its place. For all who take the sword shall perish by a sword. Or do you think that I am not able now to call on My Father, and He will place beside Me more than twelve legions of angels? How then should the Scriptures be fulfilled, that it must happen this way?”

In that hour, Yeshua said to the crowds, “Have you come out to take Me with swords and clubs, as against a plunderer? I sat with you daily teaching in the temple, and you did not lay hands on Me. But all this is happening that the Scriptures of the prophets may be fulfilled.”

Then all the disciples ran away, forsaking Him.

And those who had seized Yeshua led Him

away to Caiaphas the high priest, where the scribes and the elders were assembled. And Peter followed Him from a distance, even to the court of the high priest. And going inside, he sat with the under-officers to see the end. And the chief priests and the elders and the whole Sanhedrin looked for false testimony against Yeshua, so that they might put Him to death, but did not find any, even though there were many false witnesses coming forward, they did not find any. But at last, coming up two false witnesses said, “This One said, 'I am able to destroy the temple of God, and through three even days to build it'.”

And standing up, the high priest said to Him, “Do you answer nothing? What do these witness against you?”

But Yeshua kept silent. And answering, the high priest said to Him, “I put You on oath by the living God that You tell us if You are the Christ, the Son of God.”

Yeshua said to him, “You said it. I tell you more. From this time you shall see the Son of Man sitting off the right hand of power, and coming on the clouds of the heaven.”

Then the high priest tore his garments, saying, “He blasphemed! Why do we have any more need of witnesses? Behold, now you have heard His blasphemy. What does it seem to you?"

And answering, they said, "He is liable to death."

Then they spat in His face, and beat Him with the fist, and some slapped Him, saying, "Prophesy to us, Christ. Who is the one striking You?"

And early morning occurring, all the chief priests and the elders of the people took counsel together against Yeshua, so as to put Him to death. And binding Him, they led Him away and delivered Him to Pontius Pilate the governor. Then Judas, the one betraying Him, seeing that He was condemned, repenting, returned the thirty pieces of silver to the chief priests and the elders, saying, "I sinned, betraying innocent blood."

But they said, "What is it to us? You see to it."

And tossing the silver pieces into the temple, he left. And going away he hanged himself. And taking the pieces of silver, the chief priests said, "It is not lawful to put them into the treasury, since it is the price of blood." And taking counsel, they bought of them the potter's field, for burial for the strangers. (So that field was called Field of Blood until today.) Then was fulfilled that spoken through Jeremiah the prophet, saying,

"And I took the thirty pieces of silver, the price of Him who had been priced, on whom they of the sons of Israel set a price, and gave them for the potter's field, as the Lord directed me."

And Yeshua stood before the governor. And the governor questioned Him, saying, "Are You the King of the Jews?"

And Yeshua said to him, "You say it."

And when He was accused by the chief priests and the elders, He answered nothing. Then Pilate said to Him, "Do You not hear how many things they testify against You?"

And He did not answer him, not even to one word, so that the governor greatly marveled. And at a feast, the governor customarily released one prisoner to the crowd, whom they wished. And they had then a notable prisoner, Barabbas. Then they, having been assembled, Pilate said to them, "Whom do you wish I may release to you, Barabbas, or Yeshua being called Christ?"

For he knew they delivered Him up through envy. But as he was sitting on the judgment seat, his wife sent to him, saying, "Let nothing be to you and that just one. For I have suffered many things today by a dream because of Him."

But the chief priests and the elders

persuaded the crowds, that they should ask for Barabbas, and to destroy Yeshua. And answering, the governor said to them, "From the two, which do you wish that I release to you?"

And they said, "Barabbas."

Pilate said to them, "What then should I do to Yeshua being called Christ?"

They all say to him, "Crucify Him!"

But the governor said, "For what badness did He do?"

But they the more cried out, saying, "Crucify!"

And seeing that nothing is gained, but rather an uproar occurs, taking water, Pilate washed his hands before the crowd, saying, "I am innocent of the blood of this righteous one; you will see."

And answering, all the people said, "His blood be on us and on our children."

Then he released Barabbas to them. But having flogged Yeshua, he delivered Him up that He might be crucified. Then taking Yeshua into the praetorium, the soldiers of the governor gathered all the cohort against Him. And stripping Him, they put a scarlet cloak around Him. And plaiting a crown of thorns, they placed it on His head, and a reed in His right hand. And bowing the knee before Him, they mocked at Him, saying, “Hail, King of the Jews.”

And spitting at Him, they took the reed and struck at His head. And when they had mocked Him, they stripped off His cloak, and they put His garments on Him and led Him away to crucify Him. And going out, they found a man, a Cyrenean, named Simon. They compelled this one, that he bear His cross.

And coming to a place called Golgotha, which is called, Place of a Skull, they gave Him vinegar mingled with gall to drink. And having tasted, He would not drink. And having crucified Him, they divided His garments, casting a lot, that might be fulfilled that spoken by the prophet, "They divided My garments to themselves, and they cast a lot over My clothing."

And sitting down, they guarded Him there. And they put up over His head His charge, it having been written: “THIS IS YESHUA, THE KING OF THE JEWS.”

Then two plunderers were crucified with Him, one off the right, and one off the left of Him. But those passing by, blasphemed Him, shaking their heads, and saying, “You the one razing the temple and building it in three days, if You are the Son of God, come down from the cross."

And in the same way, the chief priests with the scribes and elders, mocking, said, "He saved others; He is not able to save Himself. If He is the King of Israel, let Him come down now from the cross, and we will believe Him. He trusted on God. Let Him rescue Him now, if He desires Him. For He said, 'I am Son of God'."

And also the plunderers crucified with Him defamed Him, saying the same. And from the sixth hour there was darkness over all the land until the ninth hour. And about the ninth hour, Yeshua cried out with a loud voice, saying, "Eli, Eli, lama sabachthani;" that is, "My God, My God, why did You forsake Me?"

And hearing, some of those standing there said, "This one calls Elijah."

Then seeing His mother, and the disciple whom He loved standing by, Yeshua said to His mother, "Woman, behold your son!"

Then He said to the disciple, "Behold, your mother!" And from that hour, the disciple took her into his own home.

After this, knowing that all things have now been finished that the Scripture be completed, Yeshua said, "I thirst."

And at once, one of them running and taking a sponge, and filling it with "vinegar," put it on a reed and "gave drink to Him." But the rest said, “Let be; let us see if Elijah is coming to save Him.”

And crying again with a loud voice, Yeshua released His spirit. And, behold! The veil of the temple was torn into two from above as far as below. And the earth quaked, and the rocks were sheared! And the tombs were opened, and many bodies of the saints who had fallen asleep were raised. And coming forth out of the tombs after His resurrection, they entered into the holy city and were revealed to many. But the centurion and those with him guarding Yeshua, seeing the earthquake and the things taking place, they feared exceedingly, saying, “Truly this One was Son of God.”

And many women were there, watching from afar off, those who followed Yeshua from Galilee, ministering to Him; among whom was Mary Magdalene, and Mary the mother of James and Joses, and the mother of the sons of Zebedee.

And evening having come, a rich man from Arimathea (Joseph by name) who also himself was discipled to Yeshua, coming up to Pilate, this one asked for the body of Yeshua. Then Pilate commanded the body to be given. And taking the body, Joseph wrapped it in clean linen, and laid it in his new tomb, which he had cut out in the rock. And rolling a great stone to the door of the tomb, he departed. And there was Mary Magdalene and the other Mary, sitting across from the grave. And on the morrow, which is after the Preparation, the chief priests and the Pharisees were assembled to Pilate, saying, "Sir, we have recalled that that deceiver while living said, 'After three days I will rise.' Therefore, command that the grave be secured until the third day, that His disciples may not come by night and steal Him away, and may say to the people, 'He is raised from the dead.' And the last deception will be worse than the first."

And Pilate said to them, "You have a guard, go away, make it as secure as you know how."

And going along with the guard, they made the grave secure, sealing the stone.

But on the first of the Sabbaths, Mary Magdalene came early to the tomb, darkness yet being on it. And she saw the stone had been removed from the tomb. Then she ran and came to Simon Peter, and to the other disciple whom Yeshua loved, and said to them, "They took away the Lord out of the tomb, and we do not know where they laid

Him."

Then Peter and the other disciple went out and came to the tomb. And the two ran together, and the other disciple ran in front more quickly than Peter and came first to the tomb. And stooping down, he saw the linens lying; however, he did not go in. Then Simon Peter came following him, and went into the tomb and saw the linens lying. And the grave cloth which was on His head was not lying with the linens, but was wrapped up in one place by itself. Therefore, then the other disciple also entered, he having come first to the tomb, even he saw and believed. For they did not yet know the Scripture, that it was necessary for Him to rise from the dead. Then the disciples went away again to themselves.

But Mary stood outside at the tomb, weeping. Then as she wept, she stooped down into the tomb. And she saw two angels in white, sitting one at the head, and one at the feet, where the body of Yeshua had lain. And they said to her, "Woman, why do you weep?"

She said to them, "Because they took away my Lord, and I do not know where they put Him."

And saying these things, she turned backward and saw Yeshua standing, and did not know that it was Yeshua. Yeshua said to her, "Woman, why do you weep? Whom do you seek?"

Thinking that it was the gardener, she said to Him, "Sir, if You carried Him away, tell me where You put Him, and I will take Him away."

Yeshua said to her, "Mary!"

Turning around, she said to Him, "Rabboni!" (that is to say, Teacher).

Yeshua said to her, "Do not touch Me, for I have not yet ascended to My Father. But go to My brothers and say to them, I am ascending to My Father and your Father, and My God, and your God."

Mary Magdalene came bringing word to the disciples that she had seen the Lord, and that He told her these things.

Then it being evening on that day, the first of the Sabbaths, and the doors having been locked where the disciples were assembled because of fear of the Jews, Yeshua came and stood in the midst and said to them, "Peace to you."

And there are also many things, whatever Yeshua did, which if they were written singly, I suppose the world itself could not contain the books having been written.

# ABOUT DARRYL W. PERRY

Darryl W. Perry is an Activist/ Author/ Comedian/ Photographer/ Philosopher/ Poet & Statesman. He was born and raised in Birmingham, AL and the surrounding area. Darryl holds an Associates Degree in Mass Communications from Jefferson State Community College and an Evangelism Degree from Link School of Ministries.

Darryl was the 2004 Libertarian Party candidate for Pennsylvania State Treasurer; 2007 candidate for Mayor of Birmingham, Alabama; 2008 Alabama Statesmen/Boston Tea Party nominee/write-in candidate for US Senate and Darryl will be running for President in 2016.

OTHER BOOKS BY DARRYL W. PERRY

1776 & Today: Why We Need A New American Revolution - ISBN:1438209452

Grey Is Not A Color - ISBN: 144140080X

Songs Of Freedom: Tales From The Revolution (editor & contributor) - ISBN: 1441402594

# ABOUT FREE PATRIOT PRESS

Free Patriot Press was founded by Darryl W. Perry in June of 2009 with the mission of "ensuring a FREE PRESS for the FREEDOM MOVEMENT" and quickly opened a Publishing Division to re-release classic books with a message of freedom and to also give new authors an avenue for publishing freedom oriented material.

The Law by: Frederic Bastiat- ISBN: 0984203710

Thomas Paine's Common Sense: Addressed to the Inhabitants of America, on the Following Interesting Subjects - ISBN: 0984203702

www.ingramcontent.com/pod-product-compliance
Lightning Source LLC
LaVergne TN
LVHW010942110826
845149LV00013B/2722
* 9 7 8 0 9 8 4 2 0 3 7 2 7 *